Praise for Beth Bentley

"Beth Bentley has always engaged her art in the interest of artists whose stories have spoken to her sense of fairness and hidden, often unrealized, talent. In *Missing Addresses* she locates herself in relation to Gerard Manley Hopkins, Anne Frank, Virginia Woolf, Van Gogh, Proust, Magritte, Kafka and Darwin.... Her writing, dense with remembered moments, blazes with sudden intensity. The little lost address book in the long final poem names those...who have fallen away or fallen behind as the poet's life carried on, resisting the winding down of all life to a rest. So the names, famous and private, become waypoints to navigate changes in the felt life of the self. And finally what are recovered are moments...of enduring purpose and depth, living deeply, passing the thermos around till it's gone, swimming at night under stars."

—PAUL HUNTER, *Breaking Ground, Mr. Brick & the Boys,* and *Stubble Field*

"How fulfilling it is to have this new collection of poetry by the late Beth Bentley and to see again how deftly she fuses lyric and narrative impulses. The poems in *Missing Addresses* draw from Bentley's passions: art and literature, germination and abatement, existence and memory. In five carefully arranged sections, the book reveals the breadth of her reflections, whether the focus is her private garden or the interior lives of Magritte, Kafka or Proust. And always, in poem after poem, her genius for metaphor shines. Here are the opening lines of 'The Old Jewish Cemetery, Prague': 'A stone village has been dropped from the sky,/ gray pointed roofs perilously tilted,/jutting upward like capsized hulls./In a crowded sea, they are their own waves,/immobilized motion.' How stunning the last phrase, how perfectly it reflects not only the magnitude of the individual poem but the magnitude of poetry itself, a magnitude displayed on every page of this remarkable book."

—LINDA BIERDS, *The Hardy Tree, Roget's Illusions,* and *First Hand*

"*Missing Addresses* holds the music, forms, astute observations, and wit of Beth Bentley's finest work. We are transported to Prague, Amsterdam, Paris, and Patagonia. Beth is a master of figurative language: 'wisteria, that fragile traveler...' ('Over Goldengrove Unleaving'). In 'An Ordinary Day in Seattle,' the poet rakes leaves, then watches a movie where bodies mimic fallen leaves: 'Khaki, with glimpses of red, they lay / as if blown there...' Her obsessions reside in systems of oppression...and the difficulties of race: 'I watched Julian learn / there's no such thing / as being half a Jew' ('Letter from Amsterdam'). This volume is, quite simply, a tour de force."

—JUDITH SKILLMAN, *House of Burnt Offerings, Premise of Light,* and *The Phoenix*

"I felt sad when I read *Missing Addresses, Poems by Beth Bentley,* because the writing is so good and because there won't be any more. Always crafted with a bit of steel and wit with surprises that stick the endings. Bentley writes in 'Over Goldengrove Unleaving': 'What is the winter for? To remember love, / wrote Roethke.' Remembering love is how Bentley leaves us. Just as with someone flipping through an old address book who sees the names of those no longer among us, an image or sound returns that resonates for a long, long time."

—SHARON HASHIMOTO, *The Crane Wife* and *More American*

"Underlying both celebration ('the smoke tree flares, the last miracle, a burning bush') and rueful lament ('I would rise and go now, but there is no Innisfree'), minor chords thrum throughout Beth Bentley's poems—of her own aging and its attendant losses, and her Jewish ancestry. While no poem is 'typical,' a characteristic poem ostensibly about a crow moves to jackboots and addresses Jeremiah—'old boy, as usual you're too late...the damage is done...' Nimble and often playful, she is never less than deadly serious. A tight, double sestina moves from idyllic scene to murder mystery to ominous meditation on rumor.... [A] fine, overdue collection."

—ANNE PITKIN, *Yellow, Winter Arguments,* and *But Still, Music*

"*Missing Addresses* begins by inhabiting familiar feelings of loss and wry hope the poet experiences when readying her garden for winter; her subjects expand ever outward to other places and people, some of whom she addresses directly and some whom she unerringly becomes. One of the most poignant (and unfortunately timeless) moments occurred for me, a fellow Jew, in the poem 'Letter from Amsterdam,' where uneasy currents from the past flow into the present and the future when, at Anne Frank's house, Bentley watches her daughter 'learn / there's no such thing / as being half a Jew.' Later, writing about Marianne Moore, Beth could be describing her poetry and herself with: 'the likelihood / of a sudden sharp slash into our banal realities.' From that startling sometimes painful cut, new ideas rise as we read, and our banal days flower into brilliance."

—SHERRY RIND, *The Storehouse of Wonder and Astonishment, Between States of Matter,* and *A Fall Out the Door*

"Beth Bentley is a major force in the Northwest school of poets, but never tied solely to the region.... She writes with sharp imagistic detail, illuminating her physical and psychological landscapes.... [She] shines light into her curious, extraordinary mind. Beauty and brutal honesty are juxtaposed; elegy, memory and intrigue follow one on the other. The world has lost a fine writer and we still hear her: 'The grown woman recalls that lighted square; / her wonder at the pure, visible world / that lives on in her... / In a country where / nothing changes, yet all is new, she moves / toward the beckoning glimmer of her real life...'"

—DAPHNE DAVIES, *Hazel's Star*

MISSING ADDRESSES

ISBN 979-8-9871521-0-2
Library of Congress Control Number: 2022949619

Front cover and frontispiece photos by Sean Bentley, inset photo anonymous
Cover and book design by Lauren Grosskopf

Pleasure Boat Studio books are available through:
Baker & Taylor, Ingram Distribution Worldwide,
Amazon.com, barnesandnoble.com
&
Pleasure Boat Studio: A Nonprofit Literary Press
www.pleasureboatstudio.com
Seattle, Washington

MISSING
ADDRESSES

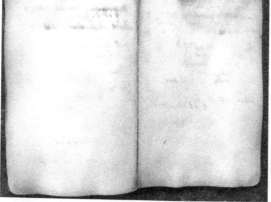

POEMS BY
BETH BENTLEY

Pleasure Boat Studio: A Nonprofit Literary Press

ACKNOWLEDGEMENTS

These poems have appeared in the following publications:

Backbone: An Ordinary Sunday in Seattle
Blue Unicorn: At Last, Patagonia
Fine Madness: To D. in Invisible Ink; Lucia; Over Goldengrove
Unleaving; Light in Autumn; The Bystanders; Missing Addresses;
La Salle des Pas Perdus; Thou Art Weighed In the Balance and Art
Found Wanting; The Old Jewish Cemetery; Nevertheless
International Poetry Review: Dying in Paris
Passages North: In the Intense Latitudes
Poetica: Two for Magritte
Poetry Texas: The Portioning
Puget Soundings: Behind You, in Boulder
Scape: Short Trip Back
Sea Pen Press: The Purely Visible

This collection was the last that Beth Bentley
had prepared for publication at the time of her death.
We dedicate it to her memory, and to the memory
of the Yarmolinskis and Singers, Blumenfelds and Klatsows,
and Lasers and Losses who preceded her and live on
within so much of her work.

Sean Bentley
Julian Bentley Edelman

CONTENTS

INTRODUCTION

"...But we are human and care with a / moody understanding / ...and you and I, / here by chance, observe them and speculate / upon their meaning... / We are silent about death. / We speak, in veiled terms, of love."
                                        —from "Euclidean Walk"

In Beth Bentley's first collection, *Phone Calls From the Dead* (1970), the title poem says: "...she has dropped the receiver; I hear only emptiness thrumming, absence...." Those who appreciate fine, engaging (and sometimes challenging) poetry may have felt the same when Bentley died in 2021. This posthumous collection, the culmination of decades of work, helps temper that absence. It gathers and reclaims an extraordinary view of the world, rendered by an inquisitive, bold, and sometimes challenging writer. I was lucky to be mentored by her, and more fortunate still to be her friend.

I met Beth by a circuitous route, as I was originally the student of her husband, the legendary University of Washington potentate of creative writing, Nelson Bentley. Although Beth never attended Nelson's "poetry workshop," she sometimes attended post-class get-togethers at a pizza joint on "The Ave." My first sight of her intimidated me; she was taciturn in the chatty gaggle, dark-haired and sharp-eyed. Eventually, she would edit and help me hone the poems of a manuscript-length collection, following my chapbook that had, fortuitously, won a Washington State award. If not for Nelson and Beth I would have quit the whole business.

Beth was instrumental, through a slowly-growing personal friendship, in pulling me from a long period of depression and heartbreak. We labored together over my manuscript, and I was a huge devotee of her work, attending many of her local readings. Once, I was even on the docket to read with her. We began to do things socially, attending readings by other writers, plays at Intiman and A.C.T., and concerts of the Philadelphia String Quartet. One of my warmest memories is of several sunny/shadowy days with Beth and her daughter, Julian, in 1972, camping on the far west coast near Rialto Beach. It's where I first became fascinated with beach stones, washed and glistening in the surf, golden and orange agates that lit up with the moving sun. Beth had brought me to a place of beauty, peace, and introspection. In January 1973, she attended an Epiphany party at my house: my journal reads, "Good to talk, later, with Beth, in the quiet of my room..." She never judged my youthful angst, she simply listened. Intently.

Beth was always writing and reading. And she traveled. Several times she took apartments in Paris for long writing sojourns. In 1977, she went for several months. With the help of a National Endowment for the Arts grant, in 1981, she was once again in Paris. I have saved a small stack of cards and letters from Paris, Florence, Prague, Rome. Reading them again, I am struck by her deep passion for learning and her interesting mind, not to mention skill in evoking place.

PARIS, JULY 30, 1977
"I have an awful fear that when I get home it will be impossible to get all the books I want to read in French. I often feel as I did two other times in my life when I simply wanted to devour whole libraries instantly.... It seems now that I'm discovering all the sources of ideas that have become so important to me the last 10 years... all the paintings and poetry here embody these ideas and I go from one to the other in a mad fury of stimulation and excitement, meanwhile struggling with the language.... I have been writing also, but, as to be expected, in totally new and different ways..."

PARIS, AUG 10, 1981
"I was lying on the couch reading, the radio on...and they began to play Franck's Sonata [for Violin and Piano]...It was gently raining outside. I was burning two candles...I had bought a bunch of flowers...a wonderfully delicate pink with many fronds—they look like constellations. Quel bonheur!... I look out the window where the canal is brownish-green, the lime and plane trees green; the alley, as always in Paris, a watery grey-blue. The light is marvelous!"

PARIS, SEPT 8, 1981
"Wonderful to receive your happy letter. Your life sounds idyllic. Funny how having to watch over a baby seems to free one from what one thought were other obligations.... Last Sunday a friend with a car took me...to visit Monet's home at Giverny.... It is fabulous, like the paintings. Fall flowers now—hundreds of dahlias, chrysanthemums, nasturtiums—a few leftover roses & clematis over arches & some late water lilies. Too late for the iris which gave so much blue & violet to his paintings."

My connection to Beth has threaded itself through so much of my time as I passed from a girl to a woman; I was probably 18 when we first met—how to characterize the force of who she is and who she has been? Beth and I suffered our losses together, too. In 1977, our fathers died within the same short few weeks. Then, when my marriage fell apart in the winter of 1990, Nelson was dying. After his death I visited Beth, alone in the house they had shared for decades, where they brought up their children.

Over the ensuing years, we saw each other infrequently as my life became busier with teaching and she navigated living alone. In 2003, I wrote to her from Ireland, where I was studying W.B. Yeats' work in a National Endowment for the Humanities seminar. Her response told me all I needed to know about how she was faring: *"...I spent a week on the Oregon coast. Perfect weather, warm and windy. No news, radio, or TV. I felt like my mind was being washed clean of this terrible year."* As time went by she suffered from a bad knee and then a knee replacement that meant she could no longer work in her beloved Seattle garden or walk around Green Lake as had been her habit.

She had published at the highest levels: *The New Yorker, The Atlantic, Paris Review,* and more, but after 1976 couldn't find a publisher for a collection of newer work. In 1998 she funded a rich, varied, and full collection, "Little Fires," through Seattle's co-op Cune Press. By 2008, she was working on what she believed would be her last manuscript.

DECEMBER, 2008
"I put together a collection and sent it everywhere last year with no takers. Been on a break from thinking about 'it' for a while, but feel I should go on trying. It's obvious the preliminary readers are all about 60 years younger than me... Old age is like living on an island, with one's contemporaries slowly disappearing without a word or even waving goodbye. I know the new year will be better for us all. Keep in touch. Love, Beth."

DEC 19, 2009
I spent most of the fall putting together a last book. I'll never have enough energy to do it again. Besides which I probably won't have enough poems of any worth to do it."

For such a tenacious and gifted writer, this must have felt like the last defeat. In the summer of 2010, I picked her up at her house and we took a drive through the fields and over the rivers of the Skagit Valley to La Conner. The tulips we could imagine in the vast fields were already finished.

During one of my visits with her, it was clear that Beth remembered less and less just as I was trying to remember her for a memoir I was writing. I pulled *Phone Calls from the Dead* from her bookshelf. She seemed to remember it. I told her what is true: she is the best poet I'd known. She pawed the air, trying to capture the words she wanted. "It's hard," she said, "when your mind is so 'creamy'... I have the words, but the words fall down the back of my throat."

A sharp mind retains a lot even as it dissolves: she was still thoughtful and reflective, seeing herself clearly, recognizing the way in which she had created silent space for her writing, space that at the end, she wandered in. She couldn't recall the word for 'paper', but she knew what she did with it; she understood that the words eluded her. She was slipping from my grasp. I keep her now in the books on my shelf, the sheaf of letters tied in ribbon.

This, Beth Bentley's ultimate collection, is rich and varied. It shines light into her curious, extraordinary mind. She explores the depth of her Jewish heritage. Beauty and brutal honesty are juxtaposed; elegy, memory, and intrigue follow one another. The world has lost a fine writer and we still hear her:

"In a country where / nothing changes, yet all is new, she moves / toward the beckoning glimmer of her real life... / ...The grown woman recalls that lighted square, / her wonder at the pure, visible world / that lives on in her."

(from "The Purely Visible")

—Daphne Enslow Davies,
November 2022

*Portions of this narrative originally appeared in a privately published memoir: Daphne H. Davies, "The Book of Good Women"; Centralia, WA, Gorham Press, 2017

I

Over Goldengrove Unleaving

As she begins to clear it, the garden
itself flaunts its decimation.
Bent pale stalks and crumpled husks
bow over mounds of ragged leavings,
discarded shells, gloves, clenched fists.

And the wisteria, that fragile traveler,
how did it come to be implicated
in the sickly branches of the rose
on its last, leggy journey? Remainders,
reminders, bite her ankles, she
who so lightly made her goodbyes.
So long, *à demain*, see you later,
à tout à l'heure. After the raking,
the clearing out, she sees
how hard the ground is, how un-
encouraging. How colorless.

To be the keeper of this is to learn
to love and let go, every
October the memory of relinquishment.
"What is the winter for? To remember love,"
wrote Roethke. Ah, how to remember
fullness, confronting these dry sticks,
these ashes hanging from the trees
like wadded handkerchiefs? She'll strew
some bulbs, just as dry, and bury them

in earth and mulch and pat them down,
putting them to bed for the winter.
It's a toss-up, for her and them, which ones
the dark and silence will bring to light.

The Blind Botanist

(A Lithograph by Ben Shahn)

He is holding the plant to his face,
grasping it with both meaty hands,
as if to feel the entire length of it,
the whole force of those thorny bracts,
from thighs, to waist, to head,
feel the essential pain prick
hands, arms, face

and his goddamned faithless eyes
which have deserted him, failing
to stay for the long haul
like a disloyal wife who couldn't cope
with the inevitable, and turned away.

His own skin reminds him
of the garden's texture, the sharp,
grainy soil, the pebbles on the path.

He lets the branches rake his cheeks,
scratch his useless eyes.
He wants to force his senses awake
as one arouses a woman, flay
his every pore. He wants his finger-pads
to paddle in small puddles of blood
until they are red as the remembered
root fronds of the plant, until
their thick, rough, wiry veins
transfuse him, restore his vision.

Miracles

And we emerge in a late afternoon hush
to leaves puttering across the pavement,
crisp as potato chips. The woodland prodigals
are living it up, painting the town red

in the driest October in decades. Our eyes
dazzle. We collect streets and yards
we never noticed before, nameless parks.
The maple on 40th and 65th
which has layered the ground with yellow,
itself its mirror. Or the line of oaks

bordering the reservoir, a sanguine haze
we drive under. And then there's that mile
from 85th to 125th
of *Fraxinus angustifolia*
some park department visionary planted
thirty years ago, a canopy
of bronzed purple, fit for a cortège;
when it turns red they call it 'claret.'

Evergreens lurk in the background
in gloomy importance; their day will come.
Who cares? We're all a little tipsy,
riding the market, squandering *gelt*
as if there were no tomorrow.

In the studio at Magnuson Park,
blinds closed to simulate darkness,
we hunch over paper, painstakingly

creating shadows in short, sharp strokes
until a white shape lifts from the page
and, out of the shadows, a perfect
transparent oval of light is born,
the image of an egg, a blown egg,
like the ones that lie before us on the table.

Outside, leaves land on our heads, weightless,
October's last legacy.
November rains begin to cull and crush
the tea-pot dregs, wash them down drains.
From a thicket of fog the smoke tree flares,
the last miracle, a burning bush.

Fraxinus angustifolia Narrow-leaved ash

Cotinus americanus American smoke tree

The Old Jewish Cemetery, Prague

A stone village has been dropped from the sky,
gray pointed roofs perilously tilted,
jutting upward like capsized hulls.
In a crowded sea, they are their own waves,
immobilized motion.

We are walking through a quarry of eloquence,
a frozen sermon, relentless
in its weight, its harsh texture.
We would like to cover our ears, our eyes,
but dare not.

The stones refuse to shift, to allow
space or air or light to invade them.
Nor, even if their designated borders
fall, would they allow one living soul
to claim kinship, shelter, comfort,

to move among them, share their sedate
wreckage. Weep though he may.

Two for Magritte

The Red Model

Are we shoes or feet?
We've been trying to remember.
What were we before we came here,
and how far have we come?
Pebbles puncture our soles
which have thinned
and are leaching into the ground.

We thought ourselves calloused,
our long memories building up
a tight shoe of resistance.
Once there were many of us,
an army of shoes, leather
moulding itself around bumps,
corns, knuckly toes,

lacing high over ankles thick as houses.
Did the soles drop off,
tattered with blind trudging,
the recalcitrance of border guards,
mountainous defiance?
Customs officials drove us off
as if we were rodents.

Some, in sympathy with their brother feet,
gradually became more pliant,
mellowing into sentience.
In this graveled and fenced enclosure

shoes and feet are one hide,
brown and misshapen. We feel the gravel
grind through our flesh, forging

red footprints, a seductive spore.

The Song of the Violet

We have come from a stony place
to a new place of stone.
As promised, these are the first stones.
God made them.
He made them to lie upon, to lie under.
The book I carry is made of stone.
I cannot put it down.
Even if I could turn the pages,
the words would be stone.
Nor can we take off our hats or coats.
We shift the furniture, stone by stone,
but it is always the same familiar stone.

Any who were children have disappeared
behind the stone walls of the city,
the stone doors.
If a violet grew here, it would be stone,
mud-yellow like a dusty star.
We thought to go to the next place
and the next, but before we could
cross the street, the places
turned to stone. Can stone injure stone?

Who would envy stone?
When stone crumbles it becomes
a base for more stones,
hardening like tears.

Letter from Amsterdam

for Jan Schmidt

1

And there we were,
latched in with those two Ilses,
the air-conditioning thick with gutturals, as the TEE
curved lovingly along the Rhine,
at every curve a village
above which a stone tower stuck,
giving us the finger.

Their faces were fortresses:
the one with cheeks like slabs
wouldn't look us in the eyes;
the other, a pale jelly,
stared at our reflections in the window
and named the castles one by one.

"Schwartze?" hissed slab-cheeks.
"Nein, nein."
The tan we got with you and Phil
at Nice still keeps us warm.

2

Achtung! at a border turned you white,
Phil said. *Schwester,*
yesterday we took a little train
2 ½ miles up the Stanserhorn.
It creaked and groaned,

crammed to the rafters with
a dozen teenage tourists from
the Fatherland, wearing flowered American
sunhats, and belting out beer-hall ballads
that cracked the cow-bells
and made the mountain shudder:
fantasies of 1930. I tried to look
American, but my face is my fortune;
my smile grew tight.

3

Along the Rhine I keep my nose
in Julian's Agatha Christie, borrowed from you,
to mute the pricking of my thumbs,
while we pass rebuilt cities, Bonn, Koln.
"Italianische?" she persists.
But when she struggles with a suitcase
big as a Volkswagen, I help her
and there are smiles all around.

"Sisters," jelly-cheeks informs me, and
indicates the other is slightly deaf.
"Swiss," she says, "Not German."
"Ah."
"Italianische?"
"No. No. American."
"Ah."

They get off happy, our differences
buried in mounds of mutual enemies.

4

Today in Anne Frank's house I turned to stone,
pretended to read the texts, then walked away,
while families of snub-nosed blonds
read every word and wrote some down.

And I watched Julian learn
there's no such thing
as being half a Jew. Her first menses
makes her matriarchal.

On Anne's wall, fading pictures of Betty Grable,
smiling children, flowers and,
in one corner, "This is why we need Israel,"
scribbled by some visitor
before these vulnerables were made
immortal with plate glass.

We walked the dog-shat streets of Amsterdam
in light I never saw in Nice,
water-filtered, clear despite gray clouds,
and saw the blue-jeaned kids
milling around the P.O. and American Express,
waiting for checks from home
to spend in little shops
on cute unnecessaries for survival.

Too young to be war-babies
they're their own cause,
and their Dutch uncles
indulge refugees.

5

When the sun fades out in Amsterdam,
only Maes and Vermeer hold the light,
canal water enough
to rim their loving with silver.
Rembrandt sinks back in gloom:
vanitas: book and bread, maps and mandolin,
hiding self-distrust with moustaches and hats.

Every day we wake to yellow hexagons
and blue diamonds on our walls,
convinced it's sunny.

Tomorrow, it's Van Gogh; he makes me cry.
But I don't need his paintings
to jog my memory: old newsreels
pressed his features onto mine
as he pressed his on Lazarus,
inmate of a death camp.
He left Rembrandt far behind,
confronting blue and yellow,
wheat and blackbirds, cypress and sun,
until they merged; no crazier
than we, though you and I
don't have to lose an ear
to prove we bleed.

6

Jan, everywhere I look I see barbed wire:
curling in sinuous hoops along the Rhine,
unrusted under glassy canal water,
sharp as crab grass among gentians
on Alpine uplands.
                   Glittering and stiff,
it springs. Jan, those loops of silver uncoil
fresh from Julian's womb and yours and mine.

Short Trip Back

I wanted to place my foot
once more on the burning sidewalk,
stalled in a Minnesota August,
thinned, pocked and feverish
with adolescence, my disease.
I wanted to suffer those years
when I pottered around the neighborhood,
a homesick explorer held captive
by the natives, worshipped
in outlandish ceremonies, kept celibate,
my untranslatable messages
smuggled out from the interior
by birds; held so long I became
like my captors, simple-minded,
chained to the wheel of food and sleep.

I was so far from my own country
I thought I had made it up:
a temperate place
where even the speech was liquid,
where one's body was a blessing,
where I could put on thought
like a skin and become whole.

Drawing Conclusions

So I'm cruising along to the tune
of my windshield wipers, rain drizzling,
urging spring on, mindless with it.
Six complicated objects to be drawn
inside boxes, he demands, desperate
for novelty, our young instructor.
The class is embedded with *dames
d'un certain age*, who are damned
if we'll admit it. One wears a velvet
beret and a scarf dangling
over one shoulder. We await his smile.
He's saving for France.

What to put in the boxes? Certainly
not that bewildered gull
borne in on a wind ten miles
from the Sound, to find himself
in a sea of cropped grass and a
claustrophobia of houses. Poets
in this neck of the woods are accused
of putting salmon, Douglas firs, seagulls
or rain in their poems. I'll draw an umbrella,
my sneakers, my beat-up old raincoat,

or Bailey, the blonde Lab,
a sweet two-year old who belongs
to a friend. Like the gull, I'm nosing
around for nourishment, beach-combing
the everydayness of my life
for that concealed shape or shadow

which in its eccentricity,
its mystery, shivers my timbers,
un pays perdu, filtered
through the overcast, a shift of light.

To D. In Invisible Ink

I will send you my poems via J.
He'll deliver them wrapped in brown paper.
On the third day of the fifth month,
following our last encounter
we'll put Plan B into operation—
but only if the lake is calm
and you can see the green boat drifting inland.

Wear the face of your sister who died
and Virginia Woolf's ivory pendant;
I'll be wearing my limp and smoking
a brown cigarillo in a holder.
I'll be painted to resemble a woman.
If there's a rose pinned to my collar,
don't speak; it means I'm being followed.
We'll switch to Plan C—unless it rains;
then I'll be under the 5th Street freeway.

I feel they're closing in;
the gloxinia's wired for sound
and a camera gleams in the laurel hedge
aimed at my bedroom window.
If J. isn't there by two
put Plan X into operation.
The capsules are in the third drawer
of the desk on the mezzanine
of the Old Towne Hotel—take the white one;
pink is my best color.

Destroy our maps, books, clothing,
all our written words;
there must be nothing left to decipher—
only our clenched bodies,
our knotted faces, our hands
made hieroglyphic by plots
and colored pencils.

I'll not contact you again,
dear sister, letter writer, favorite conspirator.

Memorize these lines. Burn this.

II

The Bystanders

It started out perfectly, the large white
dormered house drowsing above the fault-
less blue of the sea, the perfectly white
sand from which we counted sailboats, the white-
capped waves tipping the sails. We didn't see why
it couldn't go on forever. In summer white
girls drifted like moths, trailing their white
desires; each scented word dangled a clue
to linger over or follow. False clue
or real didn't seem to matter. These were the long white
littorals of summer. On the beach bodies
throbbed with the come and go of the sea's body.

One day rumors began about a dead body
washed ashore, incongruous on the white
sand as dumped debris. Although nobody
knew who had actually discovered it, nobody
confessed to it, that is, as if the fault
might be the finder's. Nor could anybody
say whose it was, what age or sex. 'The body'
we called it, in undertones, wondering why
and how it had died—murder? suicide? and why
it had washed up specifically on our beach. However, nobody
had any real information, not a clue.
Uneasily we scraped our brains for clues,

like dogs searching for forgotten bones. Clues
proliferated like bacteria. Everybody
analyzed their neighbors, inventing clues
to secret motivations that might clue

one in if one were clever. The walls of the white
house resonated, feverish with clues,
drawers opening and closing. And if clues
weren't letters, guns, cigarette butts *faute
de mieux*, we found in evasive glances and fal-
tering explanations thesauruses of clues.
Meanwhile, we pottered around discussing
why the mail came or didn't come, or why

the papers dropped the case, not that we cared why.
Mad scientists sifting microscopic clues
we worked out in sequential detail why
it was likely A and B, suspecting why
C had run from D, could have found the body,
and, if that were true, E could have said, "Why
not" to A who lied to D, and then why
they together hid an object in white
sand, it being small and colorless, white
on white concealing lie from truth. But why
was each conclusion unconvincing, fault-
ed by distrust, as if we felt the fault

might be one's own omission, a default,
one of those awful undones, painful "Why
didn't I"s, or "If only"s. Under mountains of fault-
y logic, the mystery remained unsolved. The fault,
we argued, was not in ourselves. A new clue,
a note perhaps, might turn up, restrained and fault-
lessly correct, "Forgive me—it was my own fault,"
absolving us. By then, the anonymous body,
just the fact of it, had come to embody
all our deaths, death itself, a fault-
line under the earth's crust, hardening white
scar tissue on a skin long since unwhite.

What a relief to abandon that salt-white
house, that sinister sea, a corpse bodi-
less as a ghost, the insubstantial clues,
free finally, from a crime that was no one's fault.
Though, sleepless, we lie weeping, God knows why.

An Ordinary Sunday in Seattle

In Memory of Jean Garrigue and Arthur Oberg

For two hours I pulled leaves toward me
with the long-handled rake. And the young cat leapt,
spooked at these flying claws that crackled,
yellow and red like herself.

In the light rain, for awhile, I turned my back on the world.
Hair wet, shoulders damp,
working the bamboo under blackberry and grape.
When I teased her by sprinkling leaves on her head
the cat would stalk me, tiger-eyed.

Later, at a movie, I watched actors play reporters
covering a war; it was so realistic
I forgot it was fiction. Bodies in fatigues
or camouflage clothes scattered among rubble.
Khaki, with glimpses of red, they lay
as if blown there, they had fallen so gracefully.

There were other soldiers, our own, on the evening news,
marines in desert country, clothed in the same
unobtrusive drab, to blend in with the landscape.

Except for those flown back in boxes;
the gentian and poppy-colored flags on their coffins
made a garden of color in the airy hangar;
until the cameras switched to people protesting.

*

It rains and rains, autumn in Seattle.
I soak the muscles I pulled raking.
Leaves brush the windows with a faint scream, like ghosts.
Tomorrow the children will come to the door,
ghosts holding sacks for candy.

I think of how the four of us stood in the rain,
passing the thermos back and forth.
Jean and Barbara, Arthur and I.
We sang the good songs, listened to speeches.
We had walked a long way. We felt invincible.

I remember Jean ruffling the fur
of the Obergs' white cat
while we talked about poetry in a room
made warm by wine and red rugs.
The scene fills my eyes like a color snapshot
of the heart of life, its fertile center.

*

By next week the leaves will be down.
The skinny trees will look as vulnerable as adolescents
in their uniforms of winter.
My body's ache will be deep in the bone.

The red cat will have learned to be brave;
she'll defy the ghost leaves and attack, attack.

Distemper

I listened to jazz all night;
my mind's stuffed
with the cotton wool of truisms;
even if they didn't put me to sleep.

The entire town's depressed,
replaying hours of dones and undones.
It's the wettest year since '84
or is it 1929? Whatever.

Mothers are going out of their minds
keeping their children at bay.
Quarrels and cartoons clog their ears.

I could use a local pub,
a place where I would lean on the bar
with my pals discussing
metaphysics or string theory,
chain-smoking and downing martinis—
or the latest brew.

Worldly-wise and world-weary,
we're in the second age of anxiety
or the third. Each of us with
our well-tended angst,
our semi-wisdoms.

Wisdom's out of date,
my mind's a sodden sack of lost decades.

Piles of paper on the dining-room table—
don't touch, they'll scatter!
Unanswered letters, melted wax
from last night's candles,
lit when the electricity blew,
a dozen used-up pens, rejections,
half-finished poems; ardor *interruptus*—

The storm knocked off the remaining
poppy-heads; they lie
a mess of petals, rose-silk, smeared
with the mascara of their black eyes.
And, worst of all, the smaller birds
have disappeared. Only the
Stellar jays and crows, murderers
and thieves, are on the prowl.

I'll miss the startling red of the ruddy finch;
he was primed for mating, trilling
his intricate love song one whole day
before he vanished.
Did he decide to give up his condo
and return south?

Teenagers huddle on corners
in black-hooded groups
like dissident monks
planning to overthrow the order.

I'm stuck here with my life
spread out on this disordered table.

They say the sense of smell
is the first to go.
Or is it taste?

Something is stirring the leaves
of the dogwood tree.
I would arise and go now,
but there is no Innisfree.

I Gave My Students a List of Words

Eyes
They disappeared into the mystery,
the afternoon was twenty lakes,
triste light of the mind.
The waltz, blue and gray,
ebbing, had no edges.
A mild lashing of object to element,
bird and fish fluttered in one space.

Salt
And the knives whispered to the blood
like little lies, an increase
of silver, quickening in the
environs of risk where
deadly games are played
innocently.
A pair of scissors in desire's
ballroom dances love's infancy:
none of us older than the wine.

Skin
Too tight or too loose, the mask
slips and the burglar's
nylon presses his features
into anonymity.
To be there and reveal
nothing: that is
the wall's desire.

Money
Now we're not far from that
old frontier where stories
throb in the heart's
pocket, unmistakably rhythmic.
The world lusters, trees
have metaphysical conversations.

It's chandelier time in the salons;
we're thirsty, we laugh.
Warmth is a genial jostle,
a foxtrot, a hustle.
All bodies
recognizably tribal.
For awhile.

Machine
The soured music of a doorless house,
the click of days. Regulation
that must be recognized before
it can be dismissed.
The mind invents limitations,
builds a castle with a blueprint.
The overseer with his metal smile
dictates. Only the object
has an eye, and it is glass.

Creature

Recent arrival. Ruddy from the passage,
eyelids enclosing lost warmth.
Like a train in the hold of a ship that has moved
across the channel from shore to shore,
she emerges from the rocking darkness into light,
shields her eyes from the glare, from our
looming faces. We pass her softness
from one pair of arms to another. Well,
it is a marvel to us who thought
we had finished with planting, with harvesting,
putting something new into motion. More flesh
of our flesh, familial. Though the eyes
that from some opaque knowledge rarely
rest on ours, blink and close, haven't
the least resemblance to any eyes
that we know, but are prototypical,
archetypal eyes; and the lips,
ears, hands, feet, fingers,
toes are recognizable as merely,
wonderfully human, we claim her, each
crowding around, murmuring, touching.
Then go off feeling larger, better,
comforted somehow in our inelastic
skins. We come up for air. We breathe.

III

The Purely Visible
Ten Dizains

1

The child is drunk in the library, spun
out of himself by rows and rows of books,
floor to ceiling; and the peppery dust
that teases his nose, the polish of oak
tables, their yellow smiles, the muffled years
beating against the shores of the reading-
room, the windows' wealth of light, all enter
his eyes and skin, freshly created cells,
a new limb. Summoned by words, he rises
to the ceiling, breaks through and disappears.

2

It is evening; packed snow flatters street lamps
and the sky speaks in rose to the town's roofs,
candid as shell. Marines of children
swim down the steep street, their sleds cutting wakes
in the ice, the scrape of steel crisp as fins.
At the window, a woman dries a dish
and watches them, remembering the bite
of ice, how it stings the nostrils. The taste
of fresh snow fills her mouth, and her dry cheeks
burn with the snow's gift of kisses and tears.

3

As the sky darkens, the only son takes
from the closet a jacket given to

his father as a memento by a
poet's widow. Too narrow for the older
man's shoulders, it hangs on the bones of the
boy, a brown velvet cocoon. Aware of
his aura, he moves among costumed friends,
wearing the dead man's scent like garlands
of words, his throat pleasantly caressed, his rich
curling hair singing against the collar.

4

Notes of the Czerny exercises stream
through the screen door, translating coolness from
the piano's wide throat and the room's hollows
into the sun-whitened syntax of the
flat mid-western town. The porch swing creaks with
its own weight, sprinklers whisper, serious as
metronomes, hushing the orange nasturtiums.
A gray Persian cat and a small tortoise-
shell one unsheathe the afternoon's blade; they
towel each other's faces with fierce, dry tongues.

5

A woman on a straight-backed chair hunches
over her desk, shipwrecked in a storm of
papers. On the other side of the door
the furnace heaves its underwater hide
and mutters; the windows shudder. Her pen
spends recklessly, flinging black coins seaward.
When she stops to think, her hands become shells
speaking of solitude, showing her how
her grandmother's thick gold ring clasps a blue-
white moonstone, transparent as a child's eye.

6

To the book-swimmer submerged under the
dining-room table, the blue rug on which
the sun has spilled its alphabet of dust,
the murmurs of her mother and father
in the kitchen, and the curving foot of
the table, all belong in the story.
Later, the story will have shouting from
the radio's brown maw and a harsh smell
from the kitchen where the meat is burning.
A muffled quarrel will bruise its pages.

7

He who with his first earned dimes invaded
the bookstalls, raw as a barbarian
coming away weighted down with plunder
to be dusted off, spread open, surveyed
like landscapes or oceans, that night after
night he could gallop their breadth, his vision
and longing unbridled, now lies back, eyes
closed, glasses propped on his brow, papery hands
pressing to his chest, the open book that
lies like a brooding bird come home to rest.

8

They couldn't find the baby and the grown-ups
swarmed outside, to search in the yard and street.
His little sister sniffed out his milky
scent. Trusting her near-sighted heart, she found
him asleep in the third-floor sewing-room,
curled-up like a puppy behind the door.

Now she lets the middle-aged man explain
electronics to her, his hands pale as
tubers. Behind the flat line of his voice
she sees the trees' tall houses dim their lights.

9

The little girl kneels on the sofa to
walk into the watercolor's foreign
landscape, testing the length of the rainy
road lined with brown poplar plumes. She forgets
the concrete street outside under its glaze
of ice, and the way the street's end drops down
blank as a pit. She breathes in ancestral
odors, languages. In a country where
nothing changes, yet all is new, she moves
toward the beckoning glimmer of her real life.

10

Walking home from school, brother and sister
pause to see on the bluff above the road
the fenced grounds of the Catholic orphanage.
Children in white pinafores drift like dolls,
high voices floating their questions skyward,
the black wings of the nuns ingathering.
In another climate, looking backwards,
the grown woman recalls that lighted square,
her wonder at the pure, visible world
that lives on in her, innocent of words.

The Portioning

Children, now we're under one roof,
by chance, gathered at home,
draw near. I'll unlayer
the story of my life.
In the center of this room
I'll dig a trench; you'll smell
the clear ambiguous freshness
of turned earth: compost, moisture,
roots. From the shored walls
we'll excavate bits of pottery,
a bone, a broken tooth. See,
here's the bowl of a horn spoon, and, in that crevice,
like a small, archaic eye,
glares a lopsided, hand-turned bead:
these treasures are for you.

Don't laugh. After we've graphed
and measured them, and carefully
with camel's-hair brushes cleaned
each crusted surface, uncovering
strange, crude markings, ridges,
signs of use, we'll spread them
on the table. You say this childish,
bizarre collection is the hoard
of a savage? You despise these trinkets?
Children, they're your birthright, all you get.

Pick up a piece, hold it,
rub your thumb
across the rough edges, hacked out

with more strength than skill:
feel need's rude will.
Each of you must choose what's yours.

Then bring it away from the harsh
light of the lamp, to the window
where unfiltered sun can strike.
You may detect
a scratch the chisel made,
a thumb-print on clay; or,
see where the awl slipped
and cut my hand, swirled
in the bead's cloudy gaze,
blood's pattern.

Palm the bead, child, and exit
casually but fast, hands
deep in your pockets like a thief.
Let your fingers roll
the sharp, dark glass. Feel it
pierce your skin, and feel,
in the raw sting of the cut,
your own blood surge, and burn.

He Hath Broken My Teeth with Gravel Stones

A ragpicker crow skulks outside my door,
his pallbearer coattails flapping in the wind.
He shakes his rusty forelocks and jigs a little jig.
O woe art thou, he croaks. Be warned! Beware!
Someone's rolled him in mud, his Old Testament hump
skews his bones. He mutters and limps,
yellow eyes cloudy with disaster and rheum.
Now he's leapt to the rooftree, coughing and spitting.
God, it sounds like he's wearing boots
and the boots are stomping out the doom words, the death words.
Gall! Wormwood! Ashes! Dust!
Jeremiah, old boy, as usual you're too late.
Though your rotten teeth spatter the ground, black rain,
the damage is done. The damage is done.

The Expatriate

I'm lost in the heart of Paris.
Those jungles I crossed scarred me
with their killer ants, swamps,
man-eating flowers, beetles
as big as my fist, piranhas,
silences.

The natives are suspicious and unhelpful,
reluctant to part with their
rusty hand-me-downs,
their stone dolls.
I ply them with mirrors and beads.
They hide their food from me—
I'm skin and bones.

I relinquished everything
for this doubtful happiness:
Levi-Strauss, am I richer or poorer?
This room with its drafts and sunken floorboards,
dust whimpering in corners—
what's behind the blocked fireplace?
Money, or a dead baby? I'm freezing to death—
I won't look.

Even the concièrge has better furniture,
her bird and her dog, her lace curtains
behind which she waits like a priest
for my salty confession,
which I'll make some day, out of loneliness.

Elsewhere, there's a garden like a palace,
its corridors, its rooms full of flowers:
in every salon a poet doffs his hat:
Désirez-vous?

And the river that great white way
basking like Sunset Boulevard
under the calming hands of her bridges,
caressing, caressed.
I stroke her tawny sides for hours, my languorous sister;

like Thérèse Desqueyroux, I drift
light-headed, vagrant, solitary, rapt.

Prague, Winter

Acedia

> "February, 1912...to stare at others
> with the eyes of an animal and feel
> no compunction; to yield to the non-
> conscious that you believe far away
> while it is precisely what is burning
> you; with your own hand, to throttle
> down whatever remains in you, that
> is, to enlarge the final peace of the
> graveyard and let nothing survive
> save that. A characteristic movement
> in such a condition is to run your
> little finger along your eyebrows."
>   -Franz Kafka, *Diaries*

K. is swamped in the rowboat sofa, scraping the muddy trough
of his heart; he watches the ceiling bear down
like a sinking hull. Once more, his father stumps
down the hall to the bathroom; the toilet-seat sighs and groans.

And door upon door rattles open, rusty bolts
clicking all over his skin. Private mailboxes,
their locks unfastened, spring. Click-snap. Empty.
A metallic shudder. Click-snap. Click-snap. Dead air.

Detached, his arm moves out, a contraption of pulleys
and wires; it picks up the notebook and pen, writes,
"...but to see the pages covered with things one hates,
that must be written in order for one to live!"

His father's singing invades the room, a miasma.
K. curls, a cooked sausage, sweaty, naked, taut;
he feels his body segment, slice by slice.
Flush, the toilet whispers as he slides off the sofa.

His drained parts tumble, sucked into a stream
of undifferentiated bumping refuse.
An island of dark riches floats him along
the underground sewers of Prague toward open sea.

Banal Reflections

> "Dec. 4, 1913...how could a person, even
> only as a nothing, unconsciously surrender
> himself to the nothing, and not merely to
> an empty nothing but rather to a roaring
> nothing whose nothingness consists only in
> its incomprehensibility."
> -Franz Kafka, *Diaries*

It would be simple to leave this window
where I stand splayed, a specimen
exposed to passers-by,
to leave this room with its doors
flapping open and shut, a dozen

people tramping through
like cattle in a barnyard,
mooing and muttering,
nudging me curiously.
And run headlong

out of the apartment, down the street—
that launching ramp for suicides—
toward the bridge's center,
to look down to where
the premises of the river are written.

I could inhale its pungent warranties,
the water's invitation,
follow its long grin.
How simple to grasp the lamp post
and step up onto the balustrade.

In the dip and ripple swims
the water-rat, river-colored,
only the cheerful gleam
of eye and tooth visible.
He is perfectly at home, suited

in muck.
How easily he locates his mate and meal.
His claws strip flesh from the drowned
with the calm expertise
of our cook skinning a hen.

My face dwindles at the window,
which, after all, I find
impossible to desert.
The wavering glass reviews
my pallor, my bleached assets.

At Last, Patagonia

"There, too, far away in the interior was
that place called Trapalanda, and the spirit-
guarded lake on whose margin rose the
battlements of that mysterious city which
many sought but none have found."
                    -W.H. Hudson, *Idle Days in Patagonia*

"Why, then—and the case is not peculiar to
myself—have these arid wastes taken so firm
possession of my mind?"
                    -Chas. Darwin, *Journals from HMS Beagle*

You were the ideal naturalist,
gathering birdskins methodically
to send in tattered packs to the labs.
You hoped, with a bit of luck,
to find an undiscovered species.

But that bullet in your knee slowed you.
You loitered, aimless, by the river,
and when at last you rode out,
thistle-down swirling around your shoulders,
you roamed the flat, drab pampas, a stranger.

Maybe it was those sojourns on horseback
that changed you, the sea-going motion,
wind an animal presence, carrying,
like the voices of children,
original energy.

Or was it the idle days you lounged away
under the mysterious *ombu*,
that spongy impermanence
that spirits away idea?

Once you stalked a bird so swift
no one before you had seen it.
It turned into a girl
only death could show you,
on fire in the tree top,
her urgent high sweet call
too various for transliteration.

In depleted Europe the towns you explored
were toy-size, birds like those
in primers, prototypes of birds.
You rode a bicycle, and field-glasses
brought the tame beasts closer.

The trees were just trees,
except for the beech.
In domestic soil it flourished,
familiar as an uncle.

In autumn, drawn to its earthy torso,
you were seared by its blazonry.
In that furnace of hieratic leaves
did your heart, grown luminous at last,
hear the cry of the burning girl?

Trigorin

The lake's too dark; they say it has no bottom.
It's like a stage, the firs an enclosing curtain.
Cold, too, although the servants swim in it.
Their screams rise in the air like baffled desires.
I fish from the boat, holding the pole all day,
and catch nothing. Blue-green iridescent fish
slide up and glance at me like mermaids, then flash
flirtatiously away, waggling their tails.

Who can hold a thought in the realm of water?
It shifts and sighs, reflects nine shades of gray,
confuses my eyes, my ears. Back at the house
a young girl passes in and out of airless rooms,
drifts back and forth, restless, coming and going.
She's ephemeral in her white dress, her tiny breasts
moving like wavelets under eyeletted white cotton.
Meanwhile, a dead gull putrifies on the shore,
the hole in his head black with flies and blood.

The boy plays Hamlet, his mother the guilty queen.
I've murdered no one—the metaphor peters out.
His mother tries on another Parisian bonnet,
the cost of which would support him for a month.
The rays from her icy rings weave silken leashes
that bind us to her. I'm writing a new scenario
in which a famous writer seduces a young girl
who follows him to Moscow and the theatre.

She either dies or she doesn't—I hate predictable
endings. There's an older, jealous woman, magnificently
but carelessly—what? Cruel? Indifferent? Afraid
of old age? A son who—what? Wants to be a writer?
He kills his mother's lover? The girl? Himself?
I dreamt that Nina ran into the lake. Naked,
I chased her. Afraid that the others would see my erection,
I grabbed her waist, dove deep, and pulled her under.

Lessons in Dying

For Sally, in April

Grieving, we suffer unspecified twinges;
we hurt and our X-rays show nothing.
Meanwhile, you smile, drowsy with morphine,
stayed with methadone.

Some days you're ashen, and others
the pink we're accustomed to.
Like forced cherry blossoms
transfusions color your cheeks:
"I'm fine. I feel better."

We stuff your room with flowers and balloons,
feel lightly hysterical when our jokes
make you laugh, time our visits
not to tire you, start that saw of a cough
even the tube in your lungs can't relieve.

Always, planted on your bed, the dread third,
more intimate than any of us,
the persistent suitor we hate
that you've accepted
for the only marriage you'll know.

Dear girl,
we are your bridesmaids and best men,
your matrons of honor. We're giving you away
hour by hour, your beautiful head,
downy as a young chick's, pressed to the pillow,

visibly fining to a profile on a coin,
your long bones, elegant as Ahknaton's daughters'.
One by one, we step up for your blessing,
your dry kiss, the dangerous warmth of your cheek.

Sally, while you are dying, we learn how,
like children learning a foreign language:
you teach us *le mot juste*, the pure accent
our spirits receive like breath.

Loving fills the room, and light
from the sky and the Sound: you are sleepy;
Smith Tower at night reminds you of the Parthenon;
the moon reminds you of that Easter in Brittany
driving along the coast;
the white dog that followed you,
that you brought back to Paris:
you bring us all home.

Nevertheless,

though she listed with formidable precision
the minutia of the simplest of objects
or subjects, formulating, particularizing
with a sort of cool passion, at some moment
her observations took off, as she jumped
into the ether from a standing position
embracing the airy atmosphere of the gnomic.

As if she were a creature accustomed to wild
forays in the forest of possibilities
she sailed from the literal into the tenable,
not to mention terrible. Harmless as she seemed,
her smile, benign and calm, belied the likelihood
of a sudden sharp slash into our banal realities.
She was the spiny rose we felt constrained to grasp.

In Memory of Marianne Moore

IV

The Lyrics of Summer

Yes, the broken plaster grins
on the wall, and the chairs are pushed askew
like wrong answers. The next-door's

bedroom window still thrusts
its glance into the room
where he stands, flushed and shocked,

a joke drying in his mouth,
and she's in a silver fixed glitter,
her hair rushing out into points,

a protracted crackle. The plates
are astounded under the cooling
eggs, and the knives, outclassed,

are rattled. The child stirs
with the toe of her girl-scout shoe
the shards of bottle swimming

in milk on the floor. Nothing
has changed or moved, no one's
come closer. Only the four

birch trees outside on the strip
have shuddered into leaf and have grown
in diameter; in ten minutes they've

become thirty years older.

Thou Art Weighed in the Balance
and Art Found Wanting

1611 Bible, Daniel, v. 17

Found wanting, found waiting,
waiting silently for the lost word,
le mot juste, he who for so many years
had written as fast as his pen could scratch
to keep up with the crash and waterfall

of language his mind poured forth: an eruption.
Found wandering through his well-thumbed Roget,
Webster's Ninth, the OED,
nostalgic for the quick retort, the Dorothy
Parker repartee, the Wildean epigram.

The exchange of quips, puns, digs,
elaborate insults, the flash of it,
the fun. Now settling for a flat reply
as the right word slithers away,
and someone else obligingly

fills in the blank, which is never what he
was searching for, almost had, in fact,
on the tip of his mind; he could almost see
its tail flip and vanish in a strangling rush
and clatter of glittering possibles.

He is found wanting; as one whose tongue
has lost its tastebuds, ear has lost
its drum, throat cannot open to *bel canto*.

Though he is neither deaf nor dumb,
he is found wanting, wanting back

his dear sweet mother tongue that hides,
a shy warbler, in distant, fragrant meadows.

Dying in Paris

Ah, finally the perfect
soundproof room, shuttered, too,
against the killing dust. Marcel,
I envy you. Even the yews droop
with monoxide in Father Lachaise's
dank burial ground. You have found
the one true place to write your
memoires, free from annoying visitors
and the screech of traffic. Dear boy,
do you need another muffler?
Your *prunelles* roam the cold
reaches, taking inventory
compiling statistics in the
file cabinet no one can force.

Who would have thought I'd find
somewhere with too many trees?
Even the stones are shivering,
and I cannot remember what
happened only yesterday. I wander down
to visit your fellow novelist,
Colette, under just as austere a
stone as yours, though not so grand.
Both with crosses! The cemetery cats
skulk among the rhododendrons,
sniff the ambiance and know their place,
close to Minet-Chérie and the female heart.
My Jewish brother, I scan the want-ads.
I'm still looking for my one-room flat.

In the Intense Latitudes

It is like remembering an old movie
amazed at how removed we were,
sealed in the shell of our love
like double yolks, shut away
from the passing scene, lives

of our friends mere *divertissements*.
And the ten mile drive from Ann Arbor,
in its sweltering ditch, to Silver Lake,
along country roads, almost daily,
summer upon summer, made tourists of us,
like our ancestors, stuffed
into Caddies, original spectators.

So that when the commotion down at the dock
aroused us, we sat up and gazed
from our spot on the rise, our sun-
and-water dazzle, and sleepily
watched them haul somebody
from the lake, and turn him over.

Minutes afterward, from the nearest town—
was it Monroe?—an aid car
clanged onto the secluded Eden
of our beach, followed
by an ambulance. We watched

as little boats converged
from around the lake, fish
nibbling toward bait. It was a landscaped,

a photographed life,
onlookers hushed, lake a glaze.

Until they brought a stretcher down
and lifted him, long legs dangling.
Then a woman tore loose
from the anonymous crowd
and screamed, and fought her friends.

After the ambulance and the police
pulled out, people and boats
drifted away. Even the sun
moved on, leaving its glare.
It was 5p.m., August, Michigan,
heat at its most intense.

Eventually, you and I
went back into the water
to cool off. I swam in even strokes,
far out, away, away. One, two,
breathe, one, two, breathe,
water like silk.

2
Whether it was two weeks later,
or another month, or another summer
altogether, I can't recall,
when we skidded on the long, gravel stretch
I always hated, on the way home from the lake,
sun-dazed, relaxed, in my ancient Dodge.
I was trying to pass a farmer
creeping along on his wide-bodied

tractor, when the car
simply and silently began to slide.

Far down the road, cars were coming.
One by one, they moved to the sides of the road,
mesmerized by our zigzag weave.
The easy stop at the ditch we made
in slow motion. First, the car toppled
onto its side, then, deliberately,
all the way over. We hung
upside down in our cage, trapped birds.
My glasses lay unbroken on the bank.
When we crawled out, I faced a skewed world.

I don't know how it was for you.
I skipped work the next day, though
as I remember we went to a play
that same night, the reaction delayed.

Delayed, perhaps for years,
the connection of those events
in my mind. And now you're not here
to test my memory on,
so many years, so many portents
later. I think that was the first time
I gave death, our deaths, a thought.

Lucia

(For C.E. In Memoriam)

Quando, rapito in estasi....

> "When, enraptured in ecstasy..."
> —Lucia's aria in Donizetti's opera, *Lucia di Lammermoor*

You could tell she was headed for disaster
the moment she came onstage in scene two,
rushing about in a frenzy, breasts quivering,
as she swore undying love to Edgardo.
The small boy next to me demanded,
"Now, what are they saying? It's silly!"

I wondered if you, a child hostage,
dragged night after night to the opera,
were bored by such oceanic passion,
you, in blue velvet and white stockings,
a proper little *fraulein* in Ohio.
Or did you wallow in the violin's orgasms,
the dark forebodings of the cello?

The child beside me forgets
his complaints when Lucia, forsworn,
rampages among the wedding guests.
Tough-sweet, he's rapt as a *quattrocento* angel,
while she scales the octaves of madness.
Her white nightdress is splotched with blood,
high notes blood-curdling.

Charlotte, Donizetti couldn't have penned
a more apt scenario than the one
you devised for yourself:
the *coloratura* role.

Your seasons rose and fell
to such heights and depths,
fatal encounters, betrayals,
that it seemed inevitable
when a minor character unveiled
the tragedy you staged in the wings.

Dear girl, even Lucia
returned center front to greet us
and receive her earned ovations
before the final curtain
and the flowers.

Travellers

1

The old man wavers at the edge
of his daughter's dream:
he thinks he's at the wrong address.
She goes to the window
but the sky has smudged its messages.
She remembers her childhood,
a series of windows, each
with a small girl waving
as a car vanishes around the corner
like the tail-end of a parade,
a last snatch of noise and color.
The months accordion like post-cards
from Denver, Salt Lake, Death Valley.

2

She is alone in the car, and speeding
past farms, little towns that close
their eyes. Billboards hand out
brochures like fortune cookies.
Ahead, another car, just out of sight,
distracts the grasses with its whisper.
Horizons throb from the steering wheel
into her arteries, her foot
on the pedal burns. She hunches forward

as if her body were the motor,
as if her narrowed eyes gave the engine power.
The road is blue with spent fuel.
Wait, she murmurs. Wait. I'm coming.

V

Behind You, in Boulder

(In Memory of Rolfe Humphries 1894-1969)

Student: What is the purpose of this exercise?
Humphries: To delight the class.

I slowed, slowed to a crawl,
your body formidable,
high and square,
blocking the path,
Colorado sun a stop-watch,
exposing fissures in the bricks,
the furrowed cheeks of hills,
your sunburnt neck, the thirsty

motionless trees. As if you
were stalking birds or small beasts
or trying to hear a cry
or trace freshness
in the arrested noon,

you sipped from the rare
atmosphere of that plateau
minute portions of oxygen,
a hummingbird at a feeder,
held teaspoonsful in your throat
before letting it trickle down
to the withered rooms of your lungs.

It rose, a spent wind,
with a shudder.
It was that that slowed me
behind you, in Boulder,
shadowing you,
my breath caught short,

your games forgot.
The harsh sun's glare
revealed what had been obscured
syllable-counting,
vowel-hunting,
searching for end-words.

In the cards you sent from Woodside
your last year,
their queer scribble, spaced wheezes:
"What was that alphabet game?"
"It would be fun to try a sestina backwards,"
I see what the games meant.

I imagine you at the race-track
sun blasting your bare scalp,
at the ball-park, leaning into the plays.

It is joy, fierce joy,
that makes Time hold its breath.

Sighting

He's come, then,
as if borne in on the first
battering storm, a portent of winter.
I'd been thinking about him, thinking
it was time. Looking for him,
as usual, in his favorite spot
near the boathouse.

He balances on one elegant leg,
at the far end of the dock,
himself a hieroglyph, sign
of a hut, a haystack, a shawled
and grizzled hermit: the heron
peers out across water.

The lake's adrift in lavender,
soft as a Victorian mourning veil,
shore and sky a continuum,
a stream of consciousness.
Teal float in timid flocks, the geese,
further out, giving him space.

I, too, stand apart, watching
as he contemplates his terrain,
perfectly still, indifferent to the rain
on his back, the hum of traffic.

Until a turn of his head reveals
the long, sharp beak
extended like a sensor,

sussing out the slightest modulation
of the water, a shadow, a scent.

Like him, I'm attuned to weather,
my body on the battlements of change.
Last summer I watched the lake thicken,
watched sunsets become
autumn spectaculars. Braced myself
for the shock of winter.

Now fog obliterates the lake.
It slides across the dock, the grass,
a Japanese ink-brushing.
But the heron's head dips suddenly,
snakes down as he thrusts his beak
into the water. When he lifts his head,
I see his thin neck ripple,
a brilliant blue shimmer,
as he swallows his prey.

For a moment he stands, motionless, iconic.
Then, raising his long throat skyward,
he takes off with a flourish of his massive wings,
toward the further shore, where
who knows what his suave body,
his aristocratic head, remembers.

His beak seems thinner, and his eyes,
grey slits, are hooded search-lights.
He rises, undeterred.

Lake, dock and I are diminished,
stalled in wintry silence.

Light in Autumn

I'd like to capture the reflection of the pale green sky
as I see it on the window across the room. The sky,
the real sky, is behind my shoulder if I turn
my head, in the window at my back. But against
the *faux* sky, the real (not reflected) dark green

leaves of the dogwood can be seen through the glass, leaves
almost black in contrast to the pallor of the sky.
And the real white boards of the carport structure as well
as the reflected white boards that are re-reflected
somehow from the window behind me, reflecting back

across the room, window to window, a *dédoublement*
the French might say. These doublings, these airy
refractions, on a clear September evening after
the lightest, brightest warm blue of a day,
every leaf outlined, every crevice inked in with

the narrowest of brushes, a day so light we seemed
to be treading air. Now a darkening. Gradually,
gently, the sky, mirror-clear, is reflected on glass.
Is it better to see the reflection, projection, I wonder,
rather than to watch the sky in the west as it alters?

The transparency of the sky, its transcendence, the slow
washing out of color, like water washing my eyes?
How many layers of evening could a painter uncover,
which a sky so innocently offers, and then, before
he has seen it all, so carelessly wipes away?

I watch, as I must, light fade, as it must, although there will always be an edge or sliver in the eye's corner, nesting, a reminder or memento, coming or going, about to be. I wake to its small revelation lurking behind the curtain, at the sill.

Out of Body

They waltz, seeming weightless
in their filmy white tutus
as we watch bewitched
the aquarium's private world.

They drift, transparent white strings
dangling, as they eddy up and down
in a long, wavering line,
ghostly parachutes.

They touch neither each other
or the glass in their lazy pulse,
small fists opening, closing,
nor visible mouths or eyes.

We watch, our faces pressed
to the lit enclosure,
eyes following the silent motions
of the shadow families of jellyfish.

I am afloat on my back in a Minnesota lake,
light as a leaf on the surface,
paddling gently with hands and feet
to stay here, waterborne.
I am half asleep on the surface,
all human sounds distant.
Am I water? Or am I flesh?
I lose all sense of where or when
in this virgin time.

I breathe with the children.
The vast dark room surrounds us,
the aquarium alone lit.
We're spelled in the twilight silence,
eddying lazily with the flotilla
in this contained space,

stalled in the ether, numinous.

La Salle Des Pas Perdus

This time of day one lifts or draws
the curtains to read the light,
or drifts from window to window.
Petals or flakes of snow are drifting
outside; an empty bird-feeder hangs
motionless, a broken pendulum.
Has the grass stopped growing?
Inside, rows of books, sealed
in their bright covers, close ranks,
pressed shoulder to shoulder.

A resting place to catch your breath
is what the heart both fears and longs for.
Though even here in this inert,
this inexplicable room, under your breath
your long, slow breaths say
to each other, keep coming, keep going.
Nothing's completely static
in the waiting room. You move from chair
to chair, logging time, losing time.
No two clocks tick in unison.
Nor do they indicate the exact hour.

Though you feel insular, solitary,
the place seems somehow crowded.
Not to worry. You have your ticket.
No one can do your waiting for you.

Missing Addresses

> "I'll pain my way through this."
> "Come on, my boy. How dost, my boy?
> Art cold? I'm cold myself."
>   —*King Lear*

1

When she awoke, which toward the end
was less and less, her sleep or semi-sleep
like that of the old cat her daughter kept
(she hated cats and during her daughter's
childhood wouldn't have one in the house) her lids
would open like day-lilies, petal by petal,
though without the snap that others in a
hospital bed might hear; and then they'd droop
again, yielding glimmers of indefinable color
that shifted like water, and then would lift
for an instant revealing a startle of corona,
direct and lucid as a glimpse of sky.

My little book, it's missing. I don't know.
And her lids would seal shut against her daughter
who, arrested, hovered over this new distraction,
wondering why, of all the things her mother'd lost,
being as she was now in her diminished
circumstances, reduced to a borrowed gown,
one thin ring embedded in her finger,
three hairpins, a set of teeth that slipped
out and in, it was an address book she grieved for,
as a child grieves for a disappearing balloon.

2

I thought there might be a family history clasped
in a lost book, names familiar and unfamiliar
rattle-trapping back across the country
from here on the west coast, back through the first
green legends of America, a wooden cart that pulled
the tailor and his tools, his lengths of cloth,
fine nimble fingers, spry bones. Names that backed
east and east across the Atlantic, decades
skirting France and Spain, names that bloomed
in German fields, pushed up the soil
in Lithuania, names of divided families,
separated children, the talented unstable,
the simple-minded adventurous, the *hausfrau*,
the visionary, the rabbi with five wives, scattered
over Russia, drifting down through Egypt
and Africa, a diaspora of broken connections.

3

It is the doctors who expect us to get along,
formulating some unrealistic ethic, some theory
of group responsibility, social dependency,
in airy laboratories where objects
maintain a cool separateness under blue-white
sterile light on Formica counters.
And the objects themselves are counters doctors move
as they moved patients from bed to bed,
hospital to hospital, not noticing,
or obliterating from their white houses of election,
the bewilderment of an old woman and her children,
aging, too, guilty and anxious, quarreling
among themselves over who is responsible
for a lost book, the book of memory.

4

The room's too hot or too cold,
the old woman has bent her limbs
folding herself into herself in a way
that the busy young medic just popping in
from breakfast with his wife and new infant,
clicks his eggy tongue over, trying
with clean, cool hands to unfix
the lock of her fist, lay straight
her contracted elbows and knees
into the neat rectangle of a closed case.
But she resists,
and without flexing the hinges of her eyelids,
protests: not an object.

Does she recognize the middle-aged daughter
standing at her left, whose tanned hand
smoothes the white silk pillowcase of skin
puckering over her attenuated bones?
As the bones shrink, does memory go,
flaking off page by page in a cloud of calcium?

5

And now the family has argued and demanded,
resisted and accused, and the bossy sister-in-law
has come up with what should be the iron safe
of the mother's life, like the one in your
grandfather's office that was squat and gray
and heavy with implication, though usually agape.
And the secrets are exposed, floating
upward from the old woman's fine blue hand,
an airy Palmer method skating across pages with

graceful curves and sailing slants
at a taking-off angle.

        And the names of the dead
live in cursive like Victorian dinnerware,
transparent with fragility, address after address
lightly crossed out. The mobile past shifts
its waters, layered over the serried dunes of history.
And how pale history seems, how thin,
the Kovnos and the Konigsbergs, the Odessas,
and the St. Pauls, the Dallases, the Ann Arbors.
And there you are, tracked from state to state.
And there are your children, though, even now
their addresses are obsolete.

6

Only the grandmother can give bulk to these
transparencies
which buzz and gleam, zigzagging through streaks of sun.
Between the cracks of her papery lids
glistens the colorless: is she seeing Cousin Louis,
as she claimed one day, high on lithium given her
to ward off depression, so she would eat?
Cousin Louis came and brought a troupe
of Japanese dancers, everyone was thrilled!
But where are the Hoffmans and the Shalits?
Max and Esther you remember, and Tante Yetta.
But oh, the flimsy dance of missing addresses!
Only her imagination can scumble in
dimension; another book written
to the rhythms of her parents' voices
and the Russian white of steppes, early winters
and isolated villages, the easy script

of life at a walk, when place
was as familiar as bedtime stories:

faces she can see whirling out of darkness
lit for a moment in a garden aglow
with Japanese lanterns, where a small girl
pirouettes from hand to outstretched hand,
in some suburban house, in some
never-to-be-revealed country.

7

Is it from nothing we proceed? True solitaries,
each in his own cell of the cosmic monastery,
renouncing history with our vows, making none ourselves?

Writing down, writing on water. Suppose
all the addresses were crossed out,
burnt or buried in complaisant ground,

with their misspelt names, riddled cities?
Brothers, where the little sewing room
at the top of the house? Where, then,

the 10th Street hill, the varnished toboggan
with its iron bolt mending the prow
we cracked against a tree? Space heroes,

we journeyed years, joy the spent fuel
hanging its banners like silk kites in the willows
over Minnehaha Creek; it hangs there still.

Children, narrow your eyes, address your mother's girlhood,
that disappearing planet you can secure
with the other science fiction behind

your tender lids. But you are restless,
each new set of rooms opens to the beach
of the immediate. Your bikes are silent,

foreign, fragile, built for speed. My hand's
the ancient mariner's on your thin shoulders,
my wings scrape the cell floor of this paper hive.

BETH BENTLEY'S WORK has been published in dozens of journals and anthologies, including *The New Yorker, Poetry, The Atlantic, Paris Review, Poetry Northwest, The Nation, Saturday Review, Seattle Review,* and *Fine Madness.* Her collections include: *Little Fires* (1998); *The Purely Visible* (1980); *Philosophical Investigations* (1977); *Country of Resemblances* (1976); *Field of Snow* (1973); and *Phone Calls from the Dead* (1972). Beth also selected and edited *The Selected Poems of Hazel Hall* (1980).

Her awards and honors include: Montalvo Award, 1987; Washington State Governor's Award for *Phone Calls from the Dead* and for *Country of Resemblances*; Bookseller's Award for *Phone Calls from the Dead*; and a National Endowment of the Arts fellowship, 1976/77. She was a fellow of the NEA in 1978 and that same year read at the Library of Congress. She took several trips to France in the 1970s while working on translations of contemporary French women poets. Her play about the Bronte sisters, "Speak, Radiant Angel," was produced by Seattle's Readers' Theater.

She taught poetry in the Northwest and elsewhere for over 30 years, including the course "Writing Contemporary Poetry" at the UW from 1980 to 1992. She also founded and directed the Northwest Poets' Reading Series at the Seattle Public Library from 1960 to 1974, and taught poetry to children at the Kirkland Arts League, as a Poet-in-the-Schools for Tacoma Public Schools and Lake Washington School District, and at the Cornish College of the Arts in the 1970s.

CPSIA information can be obtained
at www.ICGtesting.com
Printed in the USA
JSHW030518090323
38667JS00001B/36